A KID'S LIFE IN

COLONIAL AMERICA

SARAH MACHAJEWSKI

PowerKiDS press.

New York

Published in 2015 by The Rosen Publishing Group, Inc.
29 East 21st Street, New York, NY 10010

First Edition

Editor: Sarah Machajewski
Book Design: Michael J. Flynn

Photo Credits: Cover (colonial schoolroom), p. 17 © North Wind Picture Archives; cover, pp. 1, 3, 4, 6–12, 14, 16–18, 20–24 (background texture) Ozerina Anna/Shutterstock.com; pp. 3, 4, 6–12, 14, 16–18, 20–24 (paper) Paladin12/Shutterstock.com; p. 5 blinkblink/Shutterstock.com; p. 7 American School/The Bridgeman Art Library/Getty Images; p. 8 Stock Montage/Archive Photos/Getty Images; p. 9 Jan Tyler/iStock/Thinkstock.com; p. 11 Kasper Nymann/Shutterstock.com; p. 13 SuperStock/Getty Images; p. 15 smcfeeters/Shutterstock.com; p. 19 (church exterior) Stephen B. Goodwin/Shutterstock.com; p. 19 (church interior) jiawangkun/Shutterstock.com; p. 21 tobkatrina/Shutterstock.com; p. 22 David Smart/Shutterstock.com.

Library of Congress Cataloging-in-Publication Data

Machajewski, Sarah.
A kid's life in colonial America / by Sarah Machajewski.
p. cm. — (How kids lived)
Includes index.
ISBN 978-1-4994-0024-3 (pbk.)
ISBN 978-1-4994-0023-6 (6-pack)
ISBN 978-1-4994-0006-9 (library binding)
1. United States — Social life and customs — To 1775 — Juvenile literature. 2. United States — History — Colonial period, ca. 1600-1775 — Juvenile literature. 3. Children — United States — History — 17th century — Juvenile literature. I. Machajewski, Sarah. II. Title.
E162.M33 2015
973.2—d23

Manufactured in the United States of America

CPSIA Compliance Information: Batch #CW15PK: For Further Information contact Rosen Publishing, New York, New York at 1-800-237-9932

CONTENTS

COMING TO AMERICA

The United States' colonial period began when the first European settlers came to North America. They set up colonies that were governed by the countries the settlers came from.

In 1607, the first colonists settled in what is now Virginia. The famous Plymouth Colony was formed in present-day Massachusetts in 1620. By 1720, most of the East Coast of North America was settled with colonial towns.

Life in the **New World** was hard. Many colonists, including children, struggled to survive in a new land. Through hard work and **perseverance**, colonists shaped the country that would become the United States.

> Great Britain controlled the 13 original American colonies.

New Hampshire

Massachusetts

New York

Rhode Island

Connecticut

New Jersey

Pennsylvania

Delaware

Maryland

Virginia

North Carolina

South Carolina

Georgia

SETTLING THE NEW WORLD

Spanish **explorers** came to North America in the 1490s. The Dutch, British, and the French soon followed. The earliest settlers were **traders** who wanted to build businesses.

Soon after, **religious** groups began settling in North America. They didn't like the way they were treated in their home countries, so they left. These people saw America as a place where they could practice their religion freely.

The first settlers were mostly men. Soon, however, women and children came. The leaders believed the colonies had a better chance to succeed with whole families living there.

> Settlers felt the New World was a place where people could live however they felt best.

NATIVE PEOPLE

Native American groups lived in North America thousands of years before the colonists. Like colonial children, Native American children learned the skills they would need as adults.

COLONIAL TOWNS

Can you picture what a colonial town looked like?
Houses were made of wood. Each house had enough land to
raise animals and grow a garden. Colonial towns had a few
shops, a school, and a church. The church was usually where
government business took place.

Colonial homes had brick fireplaces. The fireplace often became the center of family life. The fire heated the house and cooked meals.

Colonial towns were full of children. Some came from Europe, but many were born in the colonies. Priscilla was a colonial girl who was born in England. Her family traveled to America and settled in the Rhode Island colony. Priscilla's parents, grandparents, aunts, uncles, and cousins lived together in one house.

RUNNING A COLONIAL HOME

Running a colonial home was a lot of work. Most things were done by hand, and everyone had a special job to do. Priscilla's father and uncle cared for their family's animals. They also planted crops, chopped firewood, and fixed tools. Priscilla's boy cousins helped so they could learn how to do these jobs.

Women's jobs were different. Priscilla's mom and aunts made the wool and **linen** used for the family's clothes. They used berries, tree bark, and walnut shells to dye the clothing. Priscilla made butter, soap, and candles for her family.

Priscilla's mom taught her how to spin thread to make cloth. Priscilla would need to know how to do this for her own family one day.

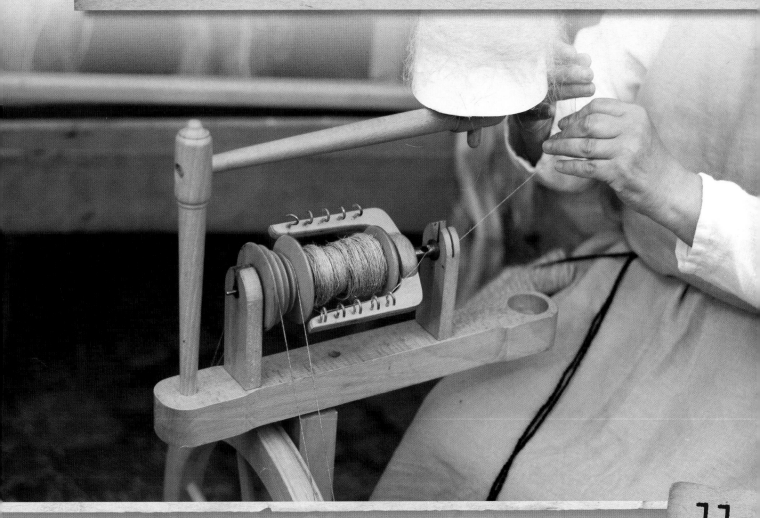

GET TO WORK!

Many colonial kids became apprentices, or people who learn a trade by working for a professional in a field for a period of time. Colonial boys became apprentices for blacksmiths, shopkeepers, and more.

COLONIAL CLOTHES

Priscilla's family wore the same kind of clothing other colonists wore. Women and girls wore long dresses with **petticoats** underneath. They wore leather shoes and caps. Men and boys wore **breeches**, long shirts, and leather shoes.

Winters were very cold in Rhode Island. Women wore hooded **cloaks** in winter. Men wore leather breeches, wool shirts, and boots. Outside, they wore coats, mittens, and hats. Staying warm was important! Many early colonists struggled through cold winters because they weren't prepared for them. Families that came later, such as Priscilla's, learned from earlier colonists how to get through winter.

This image shows the kind of clothes Priscilla and her family may have worn.

13

FARMING FOR FOOD

Colonists ate foods they could grow easily. But when the first colonists arrived in North America, they didn't know how to care for the crops that grew well there. Native Americans who were familiar with the land taught the colonists how to farm. This helped them survive.

Priscilla's family raised their own food. They grew grains, fruits, and vegetables. They raised cows, pigs, sheep, and chickens. Men hunted for deer, rabbits, and turkey. They fished, too. These foods were cooked over the fireplace in the family's home. Priscilla's favorite food was her mom's corn bread!

Corn, pumpkins, and squash were commonly eaten in the colonies. Colonists also made stews and bread.

COLONIAL SCHOOLS

Colonial children went to school in one-room schoolhouses. Most colonial schools had hard **benches** instead of desks.

Many colonial teachers felt students learned best when they **memorized** their lessons. That meant Priscilla had to remember everything she learned without looking at books to help her!

Priscilla used a hornbook for her lessons. A hornbook was a board that had the alphabet, numbers, and prayers printed on it. Priscilla was allowed to miss school if her family needed help at home.

Students of all ages were in the same classroom together. The youngest students sat in the front. The oldest students sat in the back.

SCHOOL DAYS

Colonial schools were strict. The teacher was allowed to hit a misbehaving student with a branch. A student who didn't know the lessons might have to wear a pointed hat called a dunce cap in front of the whole class.

PRACTICING THE SABBATH

Religion was a very important part of colonial life. After all, many of the earliest colonists left home in search of religious freedom.

Church leaders had a lot of control over the way people lived. They made rules about how people should dress, act, and speak.

Like most colonists, Priscilla's family attended church and observed the Sabbath. The Sabbath lasted from Saturday afternoon to Sunday night. Colonists couldn't work or play during the Sabbath. It was a time to think about their beliefs.

Priscilla had to be on her best behavior at church. She could get in a lot of trouble for being loud or not paying attention.

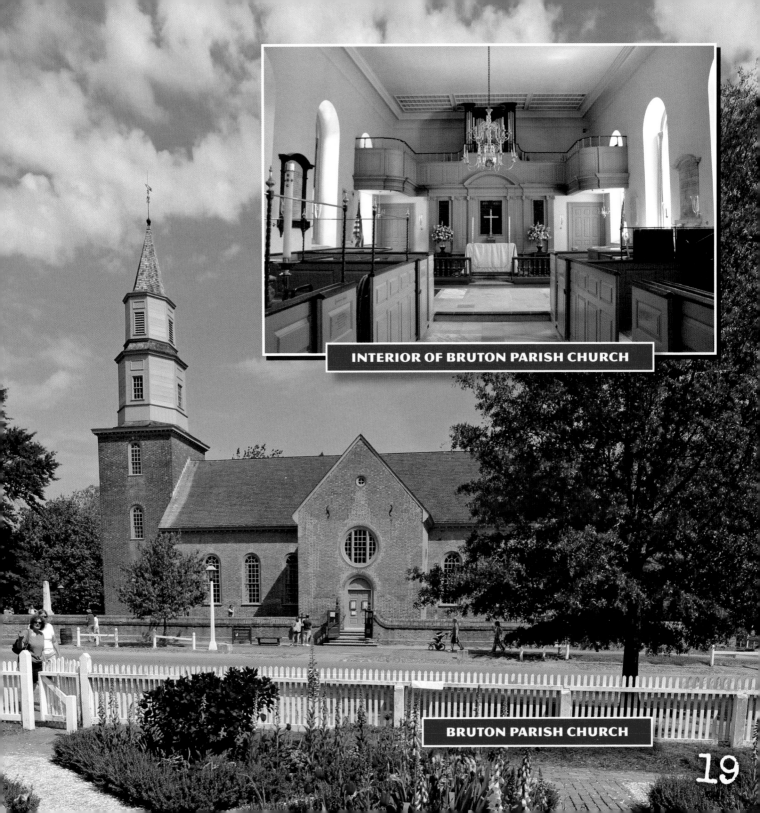

INTERIOR OF BRUTON PARISH CHURCH

BRUTON PARISH CHURCH

19

MAKING TIME FOR FUN

Colonial life involved a lot of work, but colonists liked it that way. Many believed in living a simple life of hard work. They did make time for fun, though. Events to build a new house or barn often turned into community gatherings. Men and boys liked to race. They also had shooting contests. Women went to corn **husking bees**. They also had quilting bees, where the town's women got together to make quilts.

Children had special games, too. Priscilla loved to play hopscotch. She and her friends built kites. They also played with marbles.

Priscilla and her cousins often played with puppets like the ones shown here. They loved to put on puppet shows.

TOYS FROM THE PAST

Colonial children played games that are still around today, including tag and hide-and-seek. Dolls were made from rags or leftover cloth. Many toys, such as spinning tops, were made from wood and string.

CITIZENS OF A NEW COUNTRY

The American colonies grew as more people settled there. By the late 1700s, colonists were tired of being controlled by a government that was so far away. Their ideas for how to run the colonies were different from the king of England's. He set taxes on cloth, tobacco, and other products. This made the colonists unhappy. In 1776, they **declared** their independence from Great Britain.

The 13 colonies became the United States in 1783. After the war, Priscilla, her family, and all colonists became U.S. citizens. By 1790, America's colonial period had ended.

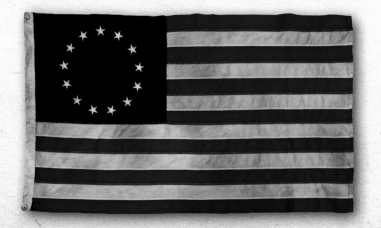

GLOSSARY

bench: A long seat for several people, commonly made of wood.

breeches: Loose pants that are fastened at the knee.

cloak: A piece of clothing worn around the shoulders that covers the whole body.

declare: To state something.

explorer: Someone who travels to find new places.

husking bee: A fun event in which people gathered to remove husks, or outer coverings, from ears of corn.

linen: A kind of cloth made from a plant called flax.

memorize: To commit to memory.

New World: A name for North and South America.

perseverance: The act of continuing to do something, even though it is hard.

petticoat: A slip worn under a skirt or dress.

religious: Having to do with believing in a god or gods.

trader: A person who buys and sells goods.

INDEX

WEBSITES

Due to the changing nature of Internet links, PowerKids Press has developed an online list of websites related to the subject of this book. This site is updated regularly. Please use this link to access the list: www.powerkidslinks.com/hkl/colo